MW00488893

THIS BOOK BELONGS TO

_____

13-Digit ISBN: 978-1-60433-841-6
10-Digit ISBN: 1-60433-841-5

This book may be ordered by mail from the publisher. Please include $5.99 for postage and handling. Please support your local bookseller first!

Books published by Cider Mill Press Book Publishers are available at special discounts for bulk purchases in the United States by corporations, institutions, and other organizations. For more information, please contact the publisher.

Cider Mill Press Book Publishers
"Where good books are ready for press"
12 Spring Street | PO Box 454
Kennebunkport, Maine 04046
Visit us on the Web! www.cidermillpress.com

The map on the cover of this notebook was originally printed in 1885 and is included for historical reference only. Please do not use the cover image for navigational purposes when exploring Yellowstone National Park.

Typography: Georgia, Hoefler Text, and Voluta Script Pro
Image Credits: All images used under official license from Shutterstock.com

Printed in China
1 2 3 4 5 6 7 8 9 0
First Edition

# YELLOWSTONE NATIONAL PARK

## SIGNATURE EDITION

**BOOK PUBLISHERS**

KENNEBUNKPORT, MAINE

# Introduction

BY OSBORNE RUSSELL
THE HUNTER'S FAREWELL
FROM *JOURNAL OF A TRAPPER; OR, NINE YEARS
RESIDENCE AMONG THE ROCKY MOUNTAINS
BETWEEN THE YEARS OF 1834 AND 1843* (1914)

Adieu ye hoary icy mantled towers
That ofttimes pierce the onward fleeting mists
Whose feet are washed by gentle summer showers
While Phoebus' rays play on your sparkling crests
The smooth green vales you seem prepared to guard
Beset with groves of ever verdant pine
Would furnish themes for Albions noble bards
Far 'bove a hunters rude unvarnish'd rhymes
Adieu ye flocks that skirt the mountains brow
And sport on banks of everliving snow
Ye timid lambs and simple harmless Ewes
Who fearless view the dread abyss below–
Oft have I watched your seeming mad career
While lightly tripping o'er those dismal heights

Or cliffs o'erhanging yawning caverns drear
Where none else treads save fowls of airy flight
Oft have I climbed those rough stupendous rocks
In search of food 'mong Nature's well fed herds
Untill I've gained the rugged mountain's top
Where Boreas reigned or feathered Monarchs soar'd
On some rude cragg projecting from the ground
I've sat a while my wearied limbs to rest
And scann'd the unsuspecting flock around
With anxious care selecting out the best
The prize obtained with slow and heavy step
Pac'd down the steep and narrow winding path
To some smooth vale where chrystal streamlets met
And skillful hands prepared a rich repast
Then hunters' jokes and merry humor'd sport
Beguiled the time enlivened every face
The hours flew fast and seemed like moments short
`Til twinkling planets told of midnights pace
But now those scenes of cheerful mirth are done
The horned [herds] are dwindling very fast
The numerous trails so deep by Bisons worn
Now teem with weeds or over grown with grass
A few gaunt Wolves now scattered or the place
Where herds since time unknown to man have fed
With lonely howls and sluggish onward pace
Tell their sad fate and where their bones are laid
Ye rugged mounts ye vales ye streams and trees
To you a hunter bids his last farewell
I'm bound for shores of distant western seas
To view far famed Multnomah's fertile vale

I'll leave these regions once famed hunting grounds
Which I perhaps again shall see no more
And follow down led by the setting sun
Or distant sound of proud Columbia's roar

*"An Act to set apart a certain Tract of Land lying near the Head-waters of the Yellowstone River as a public Park,"* signed into law by President Ulysses S. Grant (March 1, 1872).

Navy pensions, &c.

For navy pensions to invalids, widows, and dependent relatives, and pensions to sailors of the war of eighteen hundred and twelve, and for furnishing artificial limbs or apparatus for resection, with transportation or commutation therefor, compensation to pension agents, expenses of agencies, and fees for preparing vouchers and administering oaths, as provided by the acts of April twenty-third, eighteen hundred; February twentieth, eighteen hundred and forty-seven; August eleventh, eighteen hundred and forty-eight; July fourteenth and seventeenth, eighteen hundred and sixty-two; June thirtieth, eighteen hundred and sixty-four; June sixth and July twenty-fifth, eighteen hundred and sixty-six; March second, eighteen hundred and sixty-seven; July twenty-seventh, eighteen hundred and sixty-eight; June seventeenth and July eighth and eleventh, eighteen hundred and seventy, and all other pensions provided by law, four hundred and eighty thousand dollars: *Provided*, That the appropriation aforesaid for navy pensions, and the other expenditures under that head, shall be paid from the income of the navy pension fund, so far as the same may be sufficient for that purpose.

1800, ch. 33.
1847, ch. 18.
1848, ch. 155.
1862, ch. 166, 201.
1864, ch. 183.
1866, ch. 106, 235.
1867, ch. 174.
1868, ch. 264.
1870, ch. 132, 235, 238.

To be paid from income of navy fund.

Approved, February 20, 1872.

---

March 1, 1872.

1864, ch. 106, § 31.
Vol. xiii. p. 109.

CHAP. XXII. — *An Act to amend an Act entitled " An Act to provide a national Currency secured by Pledge of United States Bonds, and to provide for the Circulation and Redemption thereof," approved June third, eighteen hundred and sixty-four.*

Leavenworth stricken from the list of certain cities.

Be it enacted by the Senate and House of Representatives of the United States of America in Congress assembled, That section thirty-one of said act be amended by striking out the word " Leavenworth " when it occurs in said section.

Approved, March 1, 1872.

---

March 1, 1872.

CHAP. XXIII. — *An Act extending the Time for the Completion of the Green Bay and Sturgeon Bay and Lake Michigan Ship Canal, in the State of Wisconsin.*

Time for completing Green Bay, &c., ship canal, extended.

Be it enacted by the Senate and House of Representatives of the United States of America in Congress assembled, That the time for the completion of the Green Bay and Sturgeon Bay and Lake Michigan ship canal be, and the same is hereby, extended to the tenth day of April, anno Domini eighteen hundred and seventy-four.

Approved, March 1, 1872.

---

March 1, 1872.

CHAP. XXIV. — *An Act to set apart a certain Tract of Land lying near the Head-waters of the Yellowstone River as a public Park.*

Public park established near the head-waters of the Yellowstone River.

Boundaries.

Be it enacted by the Senate and House of Representatives of the United States of America in Congress assembled, That the tract of land in the Territories of Montana and Wyoming, lying near the head-waters of the Yellowstone river, and described as follows, to wit, commencing at the junction of Gardiner's river with the Yellowstone river, and running east to the meridian passing ten miles to the eastward of the most eastern point of Yellowstone lake; thence south along said meridian to the parallel of latitude passing ten miles south of the most southern point of Yellowstone lake; thence west along said parallel to the meridian passing fifteen miles west of the most western point of Madison lake; thence north along said meridian to the latitude of the junction of the Yellowstone and Gardiner's rivers; thence east to the place of beginning, is hereby reserved and withdrawn from settlement, occupancy, or sale under the laws of the United States, and dedicated and set apart as a public park or pleasuring-ground for the benefit and enjoyment of the people; and all persons who shall locate or settle upon or occupy the same, or any part thereof, except as hereinafter provided, shall be considered trespassers and removed therefrom.

Certain persons locating, &c., thereon. to be trespassers.

Secretary of the Interior to

Sec. 2. That said public park shall be under the exclusive control of the Secretary of the Interior, whose duty it shall be, as soon as practi-

# The parks do not belong to one state or to one section...

The Yosemite, the Yellowstone, the Grand Canyon are national properties in which

## every citizen has a vested interest;

they belong as much to the man of Massachusetts, of Michigan, of Florida, as they do to the people of California, of Wyoming, and of Arizona.

—Stephen T. Mather, first National Park Service Director
(1917-1929)

Yellowstone was the first national park, officially established on March 1, 1872, by President Ulysses S. Grant.

∾

Nathaniel P. Langford, the first superintendent of the park, held the unpaid position until 1877, though after his time spent with the Hayden Survey in 1872, he only visited the park once. This, along with a growing concern about the preservation of the land and wildlife, led to the National Park Service Organic Act, established on August 25, 1916, which resulted in the National Parks Service we know today.

∾

Yellowstone National Park takes its name from the Yellowstone River, which is the main river in the park.

*The Minnetaree tribe named the river "Mi tse a-da-zi," which means "Rock Yellow River."*

The park consists of 3,472 square miles and includes land in Wyoming, Montana, and Idaho. The elevation of the park ranges from 5,282 feet at Reese Creek to 11,358 feet at Eagle Peak. There are 1,000 miles of hiking trails throughout the park.

Average Weather Conditions:

Average Spring Temperature:
26°F to 50°F (-3°C to 10°C)

Average Summer Temperature:
44°F to 76°F (7°C to 24°C)

Average Fall Temperature:
29°F to 54°F (-2°C to 12°C)

Average Winter Temperature:
11°F to 31°F (-12°C to 1°C)

Gibbon Falls, an 84-foot waterfall, is one of hundreds of waterfalls in Yellowstone National Park.

I almost wished I could spend the remainder of my days in a place like this...

## happiness and contentment seemed to reign in wild romantic splendor

surrounded by majestic battlements which seemed to support the heavens and shut out all hostile intruders.

—Osborne Russell, *Journal of a Trapper; or, Nine Years Residence Among the Rocky Mountains Between the Years of 1834 and 1843 (1914)*

*Castle Geyser has the largest cone of any geyser in the Upper Geyser Basin and may very well be the oldest.*

From 1995 to 1996, 31 gray wolves were reintroduced to Yellowstone, marking close to 70 years since the species was removed from the area.

*There are now an estimated 528 gray wolves in the park as of 2015.*

Old Faithful is not the largest geyser in Yellowstone, but it is
the most regular. It erupts once every 51 to 120 minutes
and its spray can reach over 180 feet high.

Yellowstone has always been much more than a playground.

# It is in many ways America's holy ground—a place not only of recreation, but of creation as well—

bringing us face-to-face with the grandeur of God's works.

—Remarks by Vice President Al Gore, in his speech at the celebration of Yellowstone National Park's 125th Anniversary (August 17, 1997)

I remember being an 11-year-old kid,
first time I saw a moose in a lake.
First time we drove over a hill and
suddenly there was a field full
of deer. First time I saw a bear and
her cubs. That changes you.

# You are not the same
# after that.

—President Barack Obama, reminiscing on his first visit
to Yellowstone (June 18, 2016)

*Due to outside hunting and habitat loss, there are now less than 200 moose in Yellowstone.*

There is something in the

# wild romantic scenery of this valley

which I cannot nor will I, attempt to describe but the impressions made upon my mind . . . were such as

# time can never efface from my memory.

—Osborne Russell, *Journal of a Trapper; or, Nine Years Residence Among the Rocky Mountains Between the Years of 1834 and 1843* (1914)

I remember as a ranger the first time I stood alone on Inspiration Point over at Canyon Station looking out over this beautiful land. I thought to myself how lucky I was that my parents' and grandparents' generation had the

# vision

and the

# determination

to save it for us.

—President Gerald Ford, "Remarks at Yellowstone National Park in Wyoming" (August 29, 1976)

*Inspiration Point with the Yellowstone River below.*

Yellowstone, of all the national parks, **is the wildest and most universal in its appeal...** Daily new, always strange, ever full of change, it is Nature's wonder park.

—Susan Sessions Rugh, *Family Vacation* (2009)

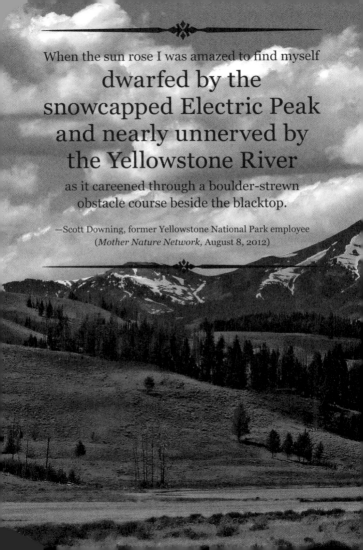

When the sun rose I was amazed to find myself **dwarfed by the snowcapped Electric Peak and nearly unnerved by the Yellowstone River** as it careened through a boulder-strewn obstacle course beside the blacktop.

—Scott Downing, former Yellowstone National Park employee
(*Mother Nature Network*, August 8, 2012)

*Electric Peak was named by Henry Gannett, whose first ascent of the mountain in 1871 was cut short by an electrical storm.*

*The tallest waterfall in Yellowstone National Park, Lower Falls, has a 308-foot drop—nearly two times the drop at Niagara Falls.*

There is something wonderful
about the wide-open spaces
that is almost a necessity
for Americans.

Being alone with
nature strengthens
our love for one
another and for
our country.

—President Gerald Ford, "Remarks at Yellowstone National Park
in Wyoming" (August 29, 1976)

[W]e came from wild land. Not too many generations back, we were hunter-gatherers ourselves. For us still to be able to even touch it from a distance and

# know that that place we came from is still safe,

that's an important spiritual concept.

—Tom Murphy, from "Never Ruin a Bear's Nap: An Interview with Wildlife Photographer Tom Murphy" (*Earthjustice*, August 2013)

Yellowstone National Park is home to about 500 geysers, which make up over 60% of the total geysers in the world.

❧

The Upper Geyser Basin has over 150 geysers per square mile, as well as hundreds of hot springs.

❧

Yellowstone National Park is situated on top of a massive super volcano, which is responsible for its unique geological and hydrological features.
There are between 1,000 to 3,000 earthquakes in and around Yellowstone per year.

*The Mammoth Hot Springs are the only major thermal feature located outside of the Yellowstone Caldera.*

National parks are no longer just scenic landscapes. They include equally compelling places that

## preserve the complicated mosaic of our history...

where we can learn and remember what it means to be an American.

—Dayton Duncan, "Are We Loving Our National Parks to Death?"
(*The New York Times*, August 6, 2016)

The Yellowstone Park is something absolutely unique in the world, so far as I know. Nowhere else in any civilized country is there to be found such a tract of

# veritable wonderland made accessible to all visitors.

—President Roosevelt, in his speech at the laying of the cornerstones for the gateway to Yellowstone National Park in Gardiner, Montana (April 24, 1903)

*Yellowstone National Park is home to the largest natural population of bison, with over 4,500 living in the park as of 2018.*

Yellowstone has 2,172 miles
of streams and rivers, and
150 named lakes.

*Yellowstone Lake sits at 7,000 feet above-sea level, making it the largest high-elevation lake in North America.*

*Yellowstone has the largest concentration of mammals in the lower 48 states, including coyotes, cougars, black bears, grizzly bears, bighorn sheep, moose, and bison.*

Yellowstone is not fixed in formaldehyde and should not be fixed in time.

# It was born in a cataclysm!

—Bob Barbee, Yellowstone National Park Superintendent
(1983-1994), (*The New York Times*, December 11, 1988)

*Great Fountain Geyser at sunset.*

Yellowstone is a wild place,
constrained imperfectly within
human-imposed limits. It's filled
with wonders of nature

# —fierce animals,
# deep canyons,
# scalding waters—

that are magnificent to behold.

—David Quammen, "Yellowstone: Wild Heart of a Continent"
(*National Geographic,* May 2016)

*There are only 14 active bald eagle nests in Yellowstone National Park.*

The wilderness that is Yellowstone Park affirms our mortality. That is why walking its trails **makes us feel so damn alive.**

—Tim Cahill, *Lost in my Own Backyard: A Walk in Yellowstone National Park* (2004)

Can we hope to preserve, in the midst of modern America, any such remnant of our continent's primordial landscape, any such sample of true wildness?...

[I]f the answer is yes, the answer is Yellowstone.

—David Quammen, "Yellowstone: Wild Heart of a Continent"
(*National Geographic*, May 2016)

Over 4 million people visit
Yellowstone National Park
each year.

YELLOWST
NATIONAL
PARK

"FOR THE BENEFIT AND
ENJOYMENT OF THE PEOPLE"

CREATED BY
ACT OF CONGRESS
MARCH 1, 1872

The Roosevelt Arch entrance to Yellowstone National Park.

# About Older Mill Press Book Publishers